FEAR FIGHTING
SCRIPTURES

31 COLORING PAGES + 31 VERSES
TO *Meditate* ON AS YOU *Color*

Debbie Hannah Skinner

ColorThroughTheBible.com
Color Through the Bible: Volume 2

Published by CreateSpace in 2017
First edition: First printing

© 2017 Debbie Hannah Skinner

Illustrations and Cover Photo by Debbie Hannah Skinner

Head shot by Alex Karber

Cover Design by Debbie Hannah Skinner and Karen R. Power

Interior Design by Karen R. Power and Debbie Hannah Skinner

Scripture quotations marked (KJV) are taken from the Holy Bible, King James Version. Public Domain.

Scripture quotations marked (WEB) are taken from the Holy Bible, World English Bible. Public Domain.

WisdomInWatercolor.com
ColorThroughTheBible.com

ISBN-978-1545232422

To all those who crave a creative outlet
for your faith in Christ.

May the time you spend
pondering Scripture as you color
strengthen, sustain, and inspire you
to live a "fear less" life.

Table of Contents

About This Coloring Book 8

The Story Behind Fear Fighting Scriptures 9

User's Guide 10

Slowly Savor the Scripture 18

In Good Company 20

The Silver Lining of Stress 21

A Few Last Thoughts 23

Genesis 15:1 25

Psalm 118:6 29

Psalm 56:3 33

Isaiah 43:1 37

Isaiah 43:5 41

Deuteronomy 31:6 45

The Tuscaloosa Tornado 49

2 Kings 6:16 51

Deuteronomy 3:22 55

Psalm 46:2 59

Isaiah 35:4 63

Psalm 27:3 67

Isaiah 41:13 71

Scripture: Our Offensive Weapon To Fight Fear 75

Daniel 10:12 77

Zephaniah 3:16-17 81

Haggai 2:5 85

Philippians 4:6 89

Psalm 139:23-24 93

Matthew 6:34 97

Stress Can Be A Signal 101

Luke 10:41-42 103

Matthew 6:27 107

Philippians 4:13 111

Romans 8:15 115

2 Timothy 1:7 119

1 John 4:18 123

Hang On Or Hand It Over 127

1 Peter 5:7 129

Proverbs 12:25 133

Ecclesiastes 11:10 137

Psalm 94:19 141

1 Peter 3:14 145

Luke 2:10 149

Joshua 1:9 153

About the Author / Artist 157

More Books By Debbie Hannah Skinner 158

Play Ground 160

A Simple Prayer

Dear Lord,
Please use the Scriptures
and coloring spaces in
this book to help our
restless hearts
release
fears and anxieties
in order to
receive
the peace that passes
all understanding
found only in
Your presence.
Amen.

About This Coloring Book

Welcome to this contemplative coloring experience. I'm so glad you are here!

This second coloring book in the Color Through The Bible series is designed to help you...

- find a new sense of focus as you meditate on Scripture while coloring
- practice "intentional abiding" in God's word
- enjoy encouragement that comes from slowly savoring powerful Scriptures, and
- cut through distractions hindering your spiritual growth

The book is filled with 31 inspirational, framable coloring pages and 31 fear fighting Scriptures for you to ponder as you color—one for each day of the month!

My hope is that with a Bible, this book, and watercolor pencils (or your favorite art supplies) in hand, you'll find a time of soul rest as you experience the anxiety-reducing joy of meditating on Scripture as you color.

-Debbie Hannah Skinner

The Story Behind Fear Fighting Scriptures

Tear drops on my computer keyboard were the last thing I expected that morning, but these words opened the flood gates:

"I struggle with anxiety. Your coloring book has helped calm my anxious mind with Scripture as I color. Thank you!"

These simple comments from a woman using my first contemplative coloring book, **Soul Soothing Scriptures**, not only made me cry, but inspired me to create this second volume on a topic that resonates with many, many people: fear and anxiety.

Why? The struggle with fear and anxiety seems to be as common as breathing these days.

A friend who serves on her church staff as a women's minister and counselor recently told me, "Debbie, you won't believe the number of women I counsel who are struggling with fear and anxiety. That one issue makes up the majority of my counseling practice." Whether it's because of shocking world events or our own personal struggles, anxiety is found everywhere we turn.

Against the backdrop of this dark news, may I gently remind you of two great facts? First, if you battle fear and anxiety you are not alone. Second, in Scripture, there's rock solid hope and help to be found in our battle with fear and anxiety.

I hope you'll see this coloring book as a creative tool to help you access that help.

User's Guide

The Tools

Gather your coloring materials. Watercolor pencils, watercolor paints, colored pencils, markers, or pens are great choices for use in this book.

Since I'm a watercolorist, I love to use **watercolor pencils** and I hope you'll try them. With watercolor pencils, once a page is colored you can use a paintbrush and tiny bit of water to activate and blend the pigment. You can also paint with water first, then color into the water for a totally different look.

Because watercolor is a transparent pigment (as compared to acrylic and oil paints which are opaque) it's great for layering color. I hope you'll give this versatile art medium a try!

Once your page dries, you can use your watercolor pencils to add other colors on top, like layers of stained glass. The colorful options are endless.

> You will find some "Play Ground" pages in back of the book where you can experiment with your art supplies and colors of choice before committing them to a coloring page.

The Time

Let's face it, everybody is busy these days. It takes effort to make space in your schedule for coloring, but I hope you discover that coloring is one of the most relaxing and releasing activities you can take part in for the benefit of your soul.

Carve out a bit of time for contemplative coloring in your schedule.

Make a coloring appointment with yourself and put it on your calendar.

I've taken my portable coloring tools to coffee shops, city parks, beside a lake, and even on an airplane. You can color just about any place once you decide to set aside the time to do it.

A Simple Technique

Ingest
(Read a Scripture verse)

Digest
(Ponder the meaning)

Write the verse
(On your coloring page)

Rest
(Meditate on the verse as you color)

Step 1: Ingest A Scripture Verse

The Bible is absolutely loaded with encouraging words that can calm our fears. Before you dive into coloring, I invite you to first dig into Scripture to look intently at the verse provided to accompany each coloring sheet.

Right before each coloring page, you'll find a Bible verse from two translations-the King James Version (KJV) and the World English Bible (WEB). These are older, public domain versions written in powerful, poetic language.

If you'd prefer to use a more modern translation of the verse, you'll also find a space where you can write that same verse from a different translation of your choice.

Once you compare the various translations of the verse, select the one you want to focus on as you're coloring.

> "Let the word of Christ
> dwell in you richly. . ."
> Colossians 3:16a

Step 2: Digest The Verse Using The "Pause To Ponder" Page

On the back of the Bible verse page, you'll find a "Pause to Ponder" page with space to think about that particular verse by **doodling** or **drawing** or **writing**.

Think of the *Pause to Ponder* page as a place for visual journaling of your thoughts and impressions in preparation for your time of contemplative coloring.

Using simple key word prompts...

Who?

What?

When?

Where?

Why?

How?

What if?

...this page is where you can spend time thinking about how the verse connects with your life right now. There's no pressure to respond to all of the key word prompts. Use as few or as many as you'd like.

Doodle or draw or write your thoughts about the connections you see. If other related or similar Bible verses come to mind, write them in this space as well.

The *Consider the Context* verses provide the larger setting for the verse you've chosen to contemplate while coloring. If you have time, I encourage you to read these passages as they can add more depth and color to your understanding of the verse.

Step 3: Write The Verse On Your Coloring Page

You'll notice one large blank space on all of the coloring sheets. That's your "Scripture space" where you'll copy–word for word–the verse you plan to contemplate as you color. (I typically write the verse using a black pen.)

> **You can mix and match coloring pages with the verses any way you'd like.** ☺

Why Write The Scripture?

There is tremendous value in writing Scripture. You can even see this in the Bible.

In the Old Testament, the Israelites were on the verge of entering the Promised Land after spending over 400 years in Egypt. Through Moses, the LORD instructed them on how they were to relate to Him and to each other as they entered in to possess this new territory.

In the book of Deuteronomy, the LORD told His people, through Moses, a day was coming when the people of Israel would have a king of their own. In Deuteronomy 17, special instructions were given in regard to how the king was to interact with God's Law...

> **18 It shall be, when he sits on the throne of his kingdom, that he shall write himself a copy of this law in a book, out of that which is before the priests the Levites. 19 It shall be with him, and he shall read from it all the days of his life; that he may learn to fear Yahweh his God, to keep all the words of this law and these statutes, to do them; 20 that his heart not be lifted up above his brothers, and that he not turn aside from the commandment, to the right hand, or to the left; to the end that he may prolong his days in his kingdom, he and his children, in the middle of Israel. Deuteronomy 17:18-20 WEB**

"He shall write himself a copy."

Isn't it interesting that God did not instruct the king to simply read a copy of the law passed down from his ancestors, written by someone else's hand? The king isn't told to ask his royal secretary to create a copy on his behalf. Instead, God commanded the king to interact with the word of God in a personal, private, and direct way—through writing.

The LORD, in His vast wisdom, instructed the king to look at the words of the law, to think about them, and then to transfer them accurately to a scroll—in his own handwriting—because of specific benefits he would receive.

> **Engaging your hands
> in doodling or writing or coloring or painting
> is a powerful way
> to be present in the moment
> and focus undivided attention
> on the LORD.**

Matthew Henry said the following about Deuteronomy 17:18 in *Matthew Henry's Commentary on the Whole Bible: Complete and Unabridged in One Volume*:

> "Though he had secretaries about him whom he might employ to write this copy, and who perhaps could write a better hand than he, yet he must do it himself, with his own hand, for the honour of the law, and that he might think no act of religion below him, to inure himself to labour and study, and especially that he might thereby be obliged to take particular notice of every part of the law and by writing it might imprint it in his mind."

This written internalization of God's word would help the king revere God, follow God's commands, keep him humble in relation to his brothers, and help him to not turn from the law. That's a whole bunch of benefits!

Likewise, as we take the time to write Scripture today, we can experience similar beautiful benefits as well.

The act of writing can help us retain information, increase our ability to focus, and cut through distractions. For many people, it's a super effective way to learn.

Writing Bible verses can help us comprehend God's word in a more complete, clear, and intimate way. Scriptures copied by our own hand are often more fresh on the mind and close to the heart, as well.

One additional benefit of writing Scripture is accuracy.

Have you ever found yourself vaguely familiar with a certain Bible verse, only to discover your paraphrase is incorrect? It's easy to leave out key words or concepts, but writing the verse can prevent this.

If you're a "skim reader" (like me), the practice of writing Bible verses can help you take note of every important component of Scripture.

Once your translation is selected and the verse is written on your coloring page, you're ready for the final step: contemplative coloring.

> "A prudent pen may go far towards making up the deficiencies of the memory, and the furnishings of the treasures of the good householder with things new and old..." - Matthew Henry

Step 4: Meditate On The Verse As You Color

Meditation is mentioned fourteen times in the Old Testament. Interestingly, the Hebrew word for meditate, *siyach*, has a very precise meaning.

According to *Biblesoft's New Exhaustive Strong's Numbers and Concordance with Expanded Greek-Hebrew Dictionary*, meditate means "to ponder, i.e. (by implication) converse (with oneself, and hence, aloud) or utter."

Do you ever talk aloud to yourself? According to this definition, that's a form of meditation, but Biblical meditation is even more.

The <u>object</u> of meditation in the Old Testament is God— His works and His ways and His word.

Many people think of meditation as the *emptying* of the mind, but Biblical meditation is actually a *filling* of the mind—with thoughts of the LORD and His word.

As you fill your mind with the remembrance of God's word, saying the words over and over to yourself (whether silently or aloud), you are practicing the Biblical meaning meditation.

My hope is that's exactly what you will do as you are coloring.

Slowly Savor the Scripture
The Potato Chip Experiment

Potato chips are one of my favorite snack foods. I've learned that when I eat them though, I have a choice to make: eat them mindlessly or mindfully.

Since I like chips so much, there have been days I've gotten carried away and eaten them super fast, a handful at a time. Staring into the bottom of an empty bag of chips one day while shaking out the last few crumbs of deliciousness and asking, "Where'd all those chips go?" I admitted I had a problem: I was eating mindlessly. (I'd eaten them all without even realizing it!)

Mindless eating usually takes place when I'm distracted by other things-like TV- or when I'm stressed or in a hurry.

Mindful eating, on the other hand, is the opposite. It's a choice to eat slowly and intentionally savor the flavors in my meal.

When I eat chips mindfully, I take smaller bites and pay close attention to all the varied flavors. I notice textures in each morsel. I go slow enough to ask myself, "Does it taste smooth? Bitter? Sweet? Salty? What about the texture? Is it crunchy? How does it feel against my teeth?"

If you're hungry, grab a bag of chips and give this a try yourself. Do the potato chip experiment and eat them with a super slow, mindful approach. You may be amazed at the difference it makes!

The intentional, mindful approach to eating potato chips has helped me learn that not all brands of chips are the same. It's also helped me cut down on the amount of chips I eat as I pause to notice the *quality* of a few over my former habit of inhaling the *quantity* of an entire bag. (My scales thank me for doing this.)

Likewise, stopping to savor Scripture in small portions in the midst of our hurried lives allows us to see and appreciate tiny nuances of flavor found in God's word instead of missing them by our busyness.

Coloring while you meditate on Bible verses-pondering the phrases, weighing the words, even repeating an entire verse to yourself as you use your hands to make art-can be a powerful spiritual practice to help you mindfully focus your attention on God's word in the present moment.

We can't meditate on Scripture in the past or future.

We can't color in the past or future.

We can only meditate on Scripture and/or color in the present.

This practice of contemplative coloring–meditating on God's word as you color–can help pull you into the present moment as you plumb the depths of meaning in Scripture.

I invite you to color mindfully.

Take your time. Savor the Scripture. Color contemplatively.

My hope is that you will experience a stressless, peaceful, colorful *oasis* time in your day as you release fear and anxiety in the process.

In Good Company

When we feel fearful or anxious, we are in very good company. Scripture makes this clear.

Throughout the Bible, we can find ordinary men and women who struggled with fear as we do today. Yet, in the midst of their stressful circumstances, God spoke to them. Giants of the faith like Abraham, Joshua, David, and Mary received words of comfort and peace in the midst of their trepidation.

Guess what? Through Scripture, the LORD continues to speak peace to us today when we are fearful.

The Silver Lining of Stress

The dark clouds of fear and anxiety can have a silver lining. I saw this illustrated through a mini-crisis on a spring afternoon several years ago.

Splashes and squeals of joyful delight rang out from the swimming pool packed with sixty or so kids. Sitting under a clear, breezy, blue Texas sky, the other field trip moms and I chatted as our kids played at their end-of-the-fifth-grade pool party.

That's when the air was pierced with my daughter's screams.

Bolting from my lawn chair, I frantically darted along the pool's edge, scanning the squirming swimmers to find her. She wasn't there.

She bellowed again.

I spun around, realizing she wasn't yelling from inside the pool, but from a grassy area outside the fence behind me. Dashing toward the gate, I broke the "no running around the pool" rule to reach her.

On approach, I realized something strange: she was howling and crying while frozen in place.

She'd sprinted outside the pool area to play with a gaggle of girls, but forgot to take along an important item in the process: her shoes. Her flip flop wearing friends had run around just fine, but not my girl. Barefoot, she had darted right into the middle of a west Texas briar patch. OUCH!

These aren't the innocent little stickers I grew up with in Alabama, the kind that would attach themselves like gentle velcro to your socks. West Texas briars are brutal. Like a ball of needles bound together with piercing points poking out in every direction, these ferocious plants can pierce skin and draw blood.

My girl was trapped right smack-dab in the middle of a briar patch the size of a parking space. (Think "bed of nails.")

Only a few steps in and she was totally stuck. She couldn't move forward or back without searing pain in her feet. All she could do was stand there howling for help.

I ran to her, lifting her slippery swimsuited body on to my back to carry her piggy back style out of the briar patch. Gently placing her on a bench, I painstakingly removed each sticker, cutting myself in the process. After several minutes, her heaving sobs ended as she finally calmed down.

I've thought about that mini-crisis many times.

Hers was an instant anxiety that day. She was running along carefree when stopped in her tracks. Sometimes our stresses are like that: sudden and severe. At other times, they come on subtly, stealthily, or, in some cases, never seem to go away, like a steady, annoying background music we can't get away from.

No matter the shape of our fears and anxieties-sudden or steady-what she did in response to her situation that day was a picture of what we can do in the midst of our distresses as well: cry out for help.

She cried out to her mortal mama that day. When we're anxious, we can do something even better: we can cry out to Almighty God!

As much as I've disliked seasons of anxiety I've walked through over the years or the dark cloud of fear that occasionally rears its ugly head in my life, I've observed a silver lining of stress. Here it is: these experiences push me into the arms of Jesus as I cry out to Him for help.

When we are in the briar patches of life, our fears can push us to cry out to the LORD and then "jump on Jesus' back" (so to speak) so He can do His brilliant, masterful work of carrying us through our distresses.

A Few Last Thoughts
(in no particular order)

Unlike many other coloring books, these designs are intentionally simple and spacious instead of being intricate and busy. That's to give you room to layer colors and textures in the spaces.

Once you finish coloring your Scripture page, you can use a craft knife or scissors to carefully remove your page.

Consider adding a mat and/or frame to your coloring sheet.

Praying a verse for a friend, then giving them the coloring page in a mat or frame, can be a great gift of encouragement.

Display your work in your home as a way to continue to meditate on God's word after your coloring session is over.

Do you have adult children? Consider sending them a sheet you have colored to hang on *their* refrigerator. ☺

Finishing this coloring book is not winning a race. There's no prize for being the first to finish. There's also no competition here.

Finally, please remember it's about the *process* of contemplating as you color, not the *product*. Be kind to yourself and enjoy the journey of engaging your hands and your heart to meditate on Scripture.

Finally, brothers,
whatever things are true,
whatever things are
honorable,
whatever things are just,
whatever things are pure,
whatever things are lovely,
whatever things are
of good report;
if there is any virtue,
and if there is any praise,
think about these things.

Philippians 4:8 (WEB)

Genesis 15:1

 After these things the word of the Lord came unto Abram in a vision, saying, Fear not, Abram: I am thy shield, and thy exceeding great reward. (KJV)

 After these things the word of Yahweh came to Abram in a vision, saying, "Don't be afraid, Abram. I am your shield, your exceedingly great reward." (WEB)

My Favorite Bible Translation of this Verse:

Pause to Ponder

Doodle . Draw . Write . Doodle . Draw . Write

Who?

What?

When?

Where?

Why?

How?

What if?

Consider the Context

Abram has left his homeland and family to follow God to a place where he has never been before.

Read Genesis 12-15.

Psalm 118:6

 The Lord is on my side; I will not fear: What can man do unto me? (KJV)

 Yahweh is on my side. I will not be afraid. What can man do to me?(WEB)

My Favorite Bible Translation of this Verse:

Pause to Ponder

Who?

What?

When?

Where?

Why?

How?

What if?

Consider the Context

The psalmist gives thanks to God for His enduring faithfulness.

Read all of Psalm 118.

Psalm 56:3

 What time I am afraid, I will trust in thee. In God I will praise his word, In God I have put my trust; I will not fear what flesh can do unto me. (KJV)

 When I am afraid, I will put my trust in you. In God, I praise his word. In God, I put my trust. I will not be afraid. What can flesh do to me? (WEB)

My Favorite Bible Translation of this Verse:

Pause to Ponder

Doodle . Draw . Write . Doodle . Draw . Write

Who?

What?

When?

Where?

Why?

How?

What if?

Consider the Context

While pursued by Saul, David runs to his enemy—the Philistines.

Read 1 Samuel 21:10-15

Isaiah 43:1

 But now thus saith the Lord that created thee, O Jacob, And he that formed thee, O Israel, Fear not: for I have redeemed thee, I have called thee by name; thou art mine. (KJV)

 But now thus says Yahweh who created you, Jacob, and he who formed you, Israel: "Don't be afraid, for I have redeemed you. I have called you by your name. You are mine." (WEB)

My Favorite Bible Translation of this Verse:

Pause to Ponder

Doodle . Draw . Write . Doodle . Draw . Write

Who?

What?

When?

Where?

Why?

How?

What if?

Consider the Context

The LORD spoke these words of hope to His people through the prophet Isaiah in the midst of the fall of the southern kingdom of Judah.

Read Isaiah 43:1-3.

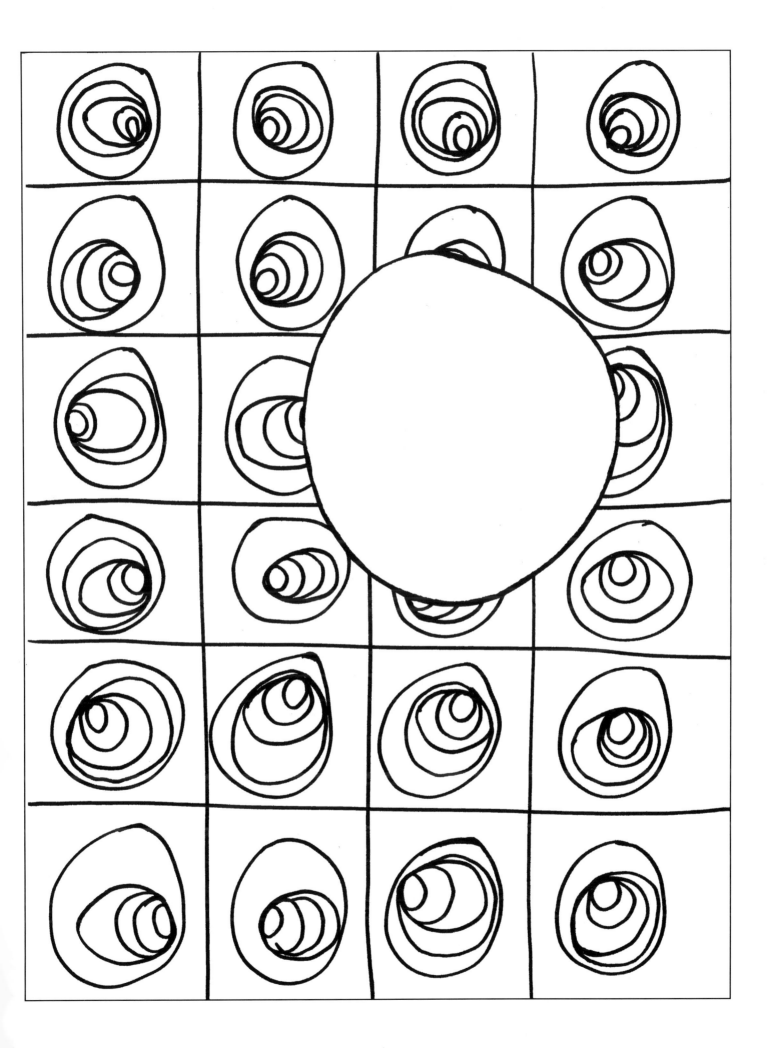

Isaiah 43:5

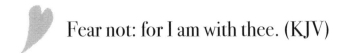 Fear not: for I am with thee. (KJV)

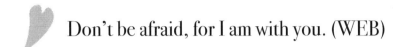 Don't be afraid, for I am with you. (WEB)

My Favorite Bible Translation of this Verse:

Pause to Ponder

Doodle . Draw . Write . Doodle . Draw . Write

Who?

What?

When?

Where?

Why?

How?

What if?

Consider the Context

The LORD spoke these words of hope to His people through the prophet Isaiah in the midst of the fall of the southern kingdom of Judah.

Read Isaiah 43:1-13.

Deuteronomy 31:6

Be strong and of good courage, fear not, nor be afraid of them: for the Lord thy God, he it is that doth go with thee; he will not fail thee, nor forsake thee. (KJV)

Be strong and courageous, don't be afraid, nor be scared of them: for Yahweh your God, he it is who does go with you; he will not fail you, nor forsake you. (WEB)

My Favorite Bible Translation of this Verse:

Pause to Ponder

Doodle . Draw . Write . Doodle . Draw . Write

Who?

What?

When?

Where?

Why?

How?

What if?

Consider the Context

Moses speaks these words of hope to his successor as he passes the mantle of leadership to Joshua.

Read Deuteronomy 31:1-8.

The Tuscaloosa Tornado
The Day Scripture Helped Fight My Fear

I'll never forget the sudden fear that signaled me to turn to Scripture on the afternoon of April 27, 2011.

Shadows danced on the grass beneath the tree branches outside the window of my home office. It was a beautiful, balmy spring afternoon in west Texas. I paused my typing mid-sentence when the phone rang. When I answered, it was my Mama in Tuscaloosa, Alabama.

Breathlessly, she said, "I'm at your sister's house. We're watching TV and can see a tornado headed this way. We're going to shelter in the pantry. Pray for us!" Click.

Over the next hours, I sat glued to my computer screen, watching news coverage of the devastating tornadoes that ripped their way across my beloved hometown and state.

A weather camera perched on top of a building in downtown Tuscaloosa recorded the monstrous storm plowing its way across the end of town where my family was hunkered down in the pantry. My heart raced as I prayed for them.

What the LORD did for me in that time of intense stress was flood my heart and mind with truth from His Word.

Six months earlier, I'd spoken at a women't ministry dinner where my text was Psalm 121. It begins like this:

**I will lift up my eyes to the hills. Where does my help come from?
My help comes from Yahweh, who made heaven and earth.**

I hadn't thought of that verse for months, but when the anxiety hit, it was immediately brought to the forefront of my mind and spilled out of my mouth. I repeated it over and over, aloud, for hours, calling out for help to the One who created heaven and earth—the One in charge of the weather!

Reciting that Scripture calmed my spirit and gave me strength in the midst of a physical and emotional storm.

Fear and anxiety came on like a bolt of lightning that day. It showed up on my door step unexpected and uninvited. All I did was answer the phone. Other times, fear is more subtle, like a lingering house guest who leaves then returns for another surprise visit.

Whether sudden or simmering, when we look at our fear and anxiety as a signal to turn to what God says to us in Scripture, it can become a gift to refocus our attention on the One who cares for us. In the process, the devastating effect of our fears can be disarmed.

My mom and sister and her family survived the tornado untouched and with only minimal damage to their property. My dad was not so fortunate. The nursing home he was in across town was in the direct path of the tornado. It was demolished. For 16 excruciating hours we didn't know if he had survived or not. Physically, he survived, but never recovered from the emotional damage of that horrible day. He died 6 weeks later, counted as a victim of the Tuscaloosa tornado.

Through those dark days of recovery after the storm, God's word continued to minister hope to me and my family.

2 Kings 6:16

 And he answered, Fear not: for they that be with us are more than they that be with them. (KJV)

 He answered, "Don't be afraid; for those who are with us are more than those who are with them." (WEB)

My Favorite Bible Translation of this Verse:

Pause to Ponder

Doodle . Draw . Write . Doodle . Draw . Write

Who?

What?

When?

Where?

Why?

How?

What if?

Consider the Context

What looks like a sure defeat of Israel by Aram is thwarted because God is on the side of Israel.

Read 2 Kings 6:8-23.

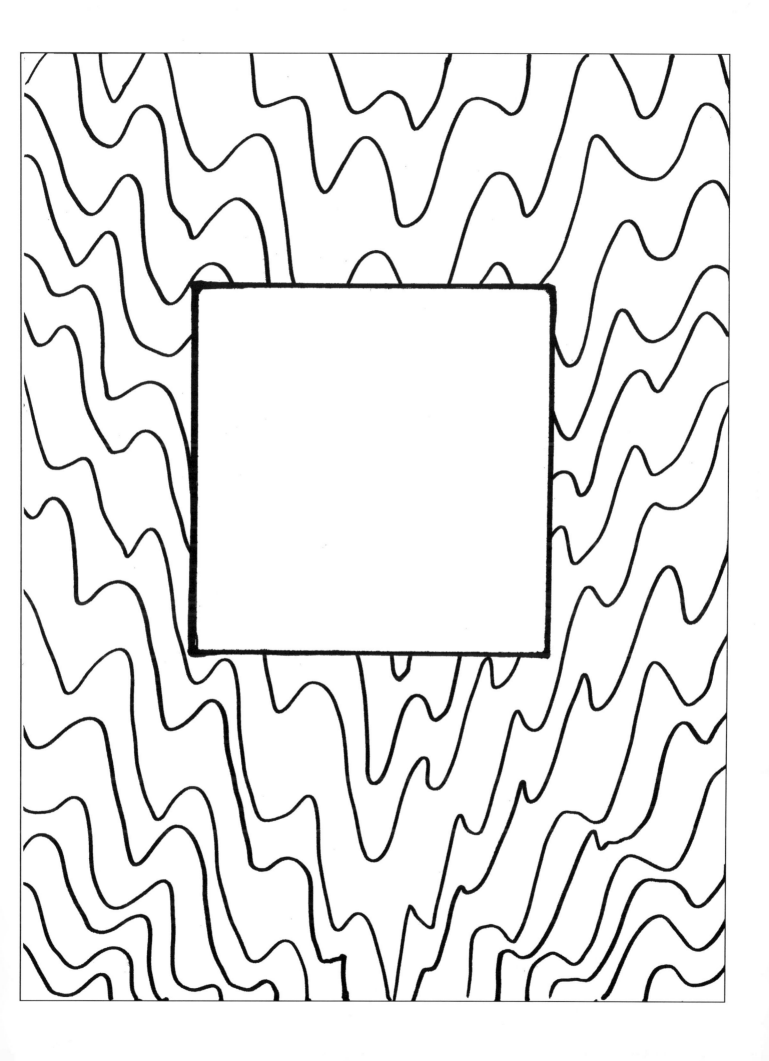

Deuteronomy 3:22

 Ye shall not fear them: for the Lord your God he shall fight for you. (KJV)

 You shall not fear them; for Yahweh your God, he it is who fights for you. (WEB)

My Favorite Bible Translation of this Verse:

Pause to Ponder

Doodle . Draw . Write . Doodle . Draw . Write

Who?

What?

When?

Where?

Why?

How?

What if?

Consider the Context

Moses cannot enter the Promised Land, but reassures his successor with words of support and strength.

Read Deuteronomy 3:21-29.

Psalm 46:2

 Therefore will not we fear, though the earth be removed, And though the mountains be carried into the midst of the sea; (KJV)

 Therefore we won't be afraid, though the earth changes, though the mountains are shaken into the heart of the seas; (WEB)

My Favorite Bible Translation of this Verse:

Pause to Ponder

Doodle . Draw . Write . Doodle . Draw . Write

Who?

What?

When?

Where?

Why?

How?

What if?

Consider the Context

God is our refuge, strength, and help.

Read all of Psalm 46.

Isaiah 35:4

 Say to them that are of a fearful heart, Be strong, fear not: Behold, your God will come with vengeance, Even God with a recompence; He will come and save. (KJV)

 Tell those who have a fearful heart, "Be strong. Don't be afraid. Behold, your God will come with vengeance, God's retribution. He will come and save you."(WEB)

My Favorite Bible Translation of this Verse:

Pause to Ponder

Doodle . Draw . Write . Doodle . Draw . Write

Who?

What?

When?

Where?

Why?

How?

What if?

Consider the Context

While under attack from enemies, David trusts God to fight for him.

Read all of Psalm 35.

Psalm 27:3

 Though an host should encamp against me, my heart shall not fear: Though war should rise against me, in this will I be confident. (KJV)

 Though an army should encamp against me, my heart shall not fear. Though war should rise against me, even then will I be confident. (WEB)

My Favorite Bible Translation of this Verse:

Pause to Ponder

Doodle . Draw . Write . Doodle . Draw . Write

Who?

What?

When?

Where?

Why?

How?

What if?

Consider the Context

David expresses confidence in God's ability to intercede for him.

Read all of Psalm 27.

Isaiah 41:13

 For I the Lord thy God will hold thy right hand, Saying unto thee, Fear not; I will help thee. (KJV)

 For I, Yahweh your God, will hold your right hand, saying to you, "Don't be afraid. I will help you." (WEB)

My Favorite Bible Translation of this Verse:

Pause to Ponder

Doodle . Draw . Write . Doodle . Draw . Write

Who?

What?

When?

Where?

Why?

How?

What if?

Consider the Context

In the midst of the looming destruction of the northern kingdom of Israel, God assures His people to "fear not."

Read all of Isaiah 41.

Scripture: Our Offensive Weapon To Fight Fear

Moses was a giant in the eyes of his people, the Hebrews. He'd led them through the Exodus from Egypt and forty years of wilderness wanderings, acting as mediator between his people and their God.

As Moses' life came to an end and a new leader was needed for the Israelites, his young assistant, Joshua, was tapped for the job. Joshua had served at Moses' side for years, but when the time came for him to lead the children of Israel to cross the Jordan River and enter the Promised Land, the massive weight of the mantle of leadership was placed on the shoulders of this young man.

Imagine for a moment the fear and anxiety the prospect of succeeding Moses could produce in Joshua. How could he fill the shoes of this great man? What if people rebelled against his leadership (as had happened with Moses)? What if he was not up to the task? What if he failed?

When faced with the daunting task of stepping into his assigned leadership position, Joshua received reassuring words from the LORD...

Joshua 1:1-9 says, Now it happened after the death of Moses the servant of Yahweh, that Yahweh spoke to Joshua the son of Nun, Moses' servant, saying, "Moses my servant is dead; now therefore arise, go over this Jordan, you, and all this people, to the land which I give to them, even to the children of Israel. I have given you every place that the sole of your foot will tread on, as I told Moses. From the wilderness, and this Lebanon, even to the great river, the river Euphrates, all the land of the Hittites, and to the great sea toward the going down of the sun, shall be your border. No man will be able to stand before you all the days of your life. As I was with Moses, so I will be with you. I will not fail you nor forsake you. Be strong and courageous; for you shall cause this people to inherit the land which I swore to their fathers to give them. Only be strong and

very courageous, to observe to do according to all the law, which Moses my servant commanded you. Don't turn from it to the right hand or to the left, that you may have good success wherever you go. This book of the law shall not depart out of your mouth, but you shall meditate on it day and night, that you may observe to do according to all that is written therein: for then you shall make your way prosperous, and then you shall have good success. Haven't I commanded you? Be strong and courageous. Don't be afraid, neither be dismayed: for Yahweh your God is with you wherever you go."

Did you notice all the things God says He has done and will do in these verses?

Make a list of those things here:

God has done this...	God will do this...

In the midst of Joshua's fear and anxiety, God promised to provide the most powerful resource in the universe to this young leader: His presence.

When we face challenges that seem too big for us to bear, are led to go to places we've never been before, are called to do jobs we feel ill equipped to handle, or feel the anxiety of living in this uncertain world, we can rest assured that the LORD says to us, as He did to Joshua, "Don't be afraid... I am with you."

Daniel 10:12

 Then said he unto me, Fear not, Daniel: for from the first day that thou didst set thine heart to understand, and to chasten thyself before thy God, thy words were heard, and I am come for thy words. (KJV)

 Then he said to me, Don't be afraid, Daniel; for from the first day that you set your heart to understand, and to humble yourself before your God, your words were heard: and I have come for your words' sake. (WEB)

My Favorite Bible Translation of this Verse:

Pause to Ponder

Doodle . Draw . Write . Doodle . Draw . Write

Who?

What?

When?

Where?

Why?

How?

What if?

Consider the Context

In the midst of the amazing story of Daniel, a young Israelite living in captivity in Babylon, the LORD hears Daniel's prayer of distress.

Read Daniel 10:1 - 11:1.

Zephaniah 3:16-17

 In that day it shall be said to Jerusalem, Fear thou not: and to Zion, Let not thine hands be slack. The Lord thy God in the midst of thee is mighty; he will save, he will rejoice over thee with joy; he will rest in his love, he will joy over thee with singing. (KJV)

 In that day, it will be said to Jerusalem, "Don't be afraid, Zion. Don't let your hands be weak." Yahweh, your God, is in the midst of you, a mighty one who will save. He will rejoice over you wth joy. He will calm you in his love. He will rejoice over you with singing. (WEB)

My Favorite Bible Translation of this Verse:

Pause to Ponder

Doodle . Draw . Write . Doodle . Draw . Write

Who?

What?

When?

Where?

Why?

How?

What if?

Consider the Context

The short book of Zephaniah is a prophecy about dark times to come for God's enemies. In the midst of the bleak message, verses 16-17 in chapter 3 stand out like a candle glowing on a dark night.

Read Zephaniah 1-3.

Haggai 2:5

 According to the word that I covenanted with you when ye came out of Egypt, so my spirit remaineth among you: fear ye not. (KJV)

 This is the word that I covenanted with you when you came out of Egypt, and my Spirit lived among you. "Don't be afraid." (WEB)

My Favorite Bible Translation of this Verse:

Pause to Ponder

Doodle . Draw . Write . Doodle . Draw . Write

Who?

What?

When?

Where?

Why?

How?

What if?

Consider the Context

God reminds His people He has promised His presence will stay with them.

Read Haggai 1-2.

Philippians 4:6

 Be careful for nothing; but in every thing by prayer and supplication with thanksgiving let your requests be made known unto God. (KJV)

 In nothing be anxious, but in everything, by prayer and petition with thanksgiving, let your requests be made known to God. (WEB)

My Favorite Bible Translation of this Verse:

Pause to Ponder

Doodle . Draw . Write . Doodle . Draw . Write

Who?

What?

When?

Where?

Why?

How?

What if?

Consider the Context

Written during his time of imprisonment, Paul reminds the church in Philippi to not be anxious.

Read Philippians 4:4-9.

Psalm 139:23-24

 Search me, O God, and know my heart: try me, and know my thoughts: And see if there be any wicked way in me, and lead me in the way everlasting. (KJV)

 Search me, God, and know my heart. Try me, and know my thoughts. See if there is any wicked way in me, and lead me in the everlasting way. (WEB)

My Favorite Bible Translation of this Verse:

Pause to Ponder

Who?

What?

When?

Where?

Why?

How?

What if?

Consider the Context

Consider David's beautiful words about God's intimate, loving knowledge of His people.

Read all of Psalm 139.

Matthew 6:34

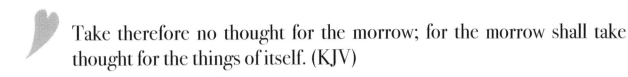 Take therefore no thought for the morrow; for the morrow shall take thought for the things of itself. (KJV)

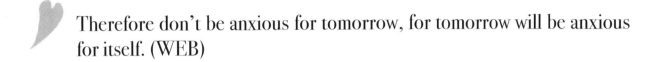 Therefore don't be anxious for tomorrow, for tomorrow will be anxious for itself. (WEB)

My Favorite Bible Translation of this Verse:

Pause to Ponder

Doodle . Draw . Write . Doodle . Draw . Write

Who?

What?

When?

Where?

Why?

How?

What if?

Consider the Context

In the context of His Sermon on the Mount, Jesus addresses the need to not be anxious or worried.

Read Matthew 6:25-34.

Stress Can Be A Signal

During my years as a public school teacher, I noticed the most effective teachers were those skilled in two areas: their subject content matter and classroom management. You could not have one without the other. One particular teacher, my friend, Laura, was a genius classroom manager, particularly with her use of signals. Let me explain. . .

Signals are prearranged gestures or sounds teachers use to elicit specific behaviors from their students. They are especially helpful in guiding students to transition from one activity to the next.

When it was time for students to move from one activity to another throughout the school day, I watched Laura use a simple hand signal to let them know it was time to move. If the class was getting too loud, she would clap in a rhythmic pattern, making a sound signal her students would repeat back to her. Soon their chatter was replaced by clapping and she had their attention.

At other times, off task students were refocused on the lesson by a simple signal of Laura stopping mid sentence and pointing to her eyes, a gesture her students were trained to mimic. The simple move would refocus their attention on her. Laura's signals were brilliant and her smooth running classroom was the fruit of her labor.

Have you ever considered that our feelings of fear and anxiety can be "signals"? They can actually be pointers that capture our attention and help us turn to God and His word for hope and help.

If anyone experienced stress in Scripture, it was Moses and the Israelite people as they made their exodus from Egypt. I cannot imagine the shudders of sheer terror that rolled through camp when, at one point, every place they looked seemed hopeless.

Ahead lay sure death by drowning in the Red Sea. Breathing down their neck, from behind, was death by sword at the hands of Pharaoh's troops.

In the midst of their anxiety, here's what happened...

When Pharaoh drew near, the children of Israel lifted up their eyes, and behold, the Egyptians were marching after them; and they were very afraid. The children of Israel cried out to Yahweh. They said to Moses, "Because there were no graves in Egypt, have you taken us away to die in the wilderness? Why have you treated us this way, to bring us forth out of Egypt? Isn't this the word that we spoke to you in Egypt, saying, 'Leave us alone, that we may serve the Egyptians?' For it were better for us to serve the Egyptians, than that we should die in the wilderness." Moses said to the people, "Don't be afraid. Stand still, and see the salvation of Yahweh, which he will work for you today: for the Egyptians whom you have seen today, you shall never see them again. Yahweh will fight for you, and you shall be still." Exodus 14:10-14 WEB

Moses reminded his terrified people to not fear but trust God. How? Simply be still and watch the Lord fight on their behalf.

It was as though their stress was a signal from God to not peer in panic at their surroundings but to focus in faith on their Savior instead.

Exodus 14 tells the miraculous story of how God moved on their behalf. Through divine intervention, the massive sea was parted. The Israelites walked across on dry land. Pursuing Egyptian enemies were destroyed. God showed up in a huge way that day to supernaturally deliver His chosen people.

The next time a stressor comes along, stop and consider that it could be a signal to do what the Israelites were told to do: stop, refuse to fear, be still, and look to the Lord to fight on your behalf.

Luke 10:41-42

 And Jesus answered and said unto her, Martha, Martha, thou art careful and troubled about many things: But one thing is needful: and Mary hath chosen that good part, which shall not be taken away from her. (KJV)

 Jesus answered her, "Martha, Martha, you are anxious and troubled about many things, but one thing is needed. Mary has chosen the good part, which will not be taken away from her." (WEB)

My Favorite Bible Translation of this Verse:

Pause to Ponder

Doodle . Draw . Write . Doodle . Draw . Write

Who?

What?

When?

Where?

Why?

How?

What if?

Consider the Context

Jesus visits the home of His friends Mary, Martha, and Lazarus. Martha is stressing over her service while Mary sits at Jesus' feet, listening.

Read Luke 10:38-42.

Matthew 6:27

 Which of you by taking thought can add one cubit unto his stature? (KJV)

 Which of you, by being anxious can add one moment to his lifespan? (WEB)

My Favorite Bible Translation of this Verse:

Pause to Ponder
Doodle . Draw . Write . Doodle . Draw . Write

Who?

What?

When?

Where?

Why?

How?

What if?

Consider the Context

Jesus speaks of the pointlessness of hanging on to anxiety.

Read Matthew 6:25-34.

Philippians 4:13

 I can do all things through Christ which strengtheneth me. (KJV)

 I can do all things through Christ, who strengthens me. (WEB)

My Favorite Bible Translation of this Verse:

Pause to Ponder

Doodle . Draw . Write . Doodle . Draw . Write

Who?

What?

When?

Where?

Why?

How?

What if?

Consider the Context

Written from prison, Paul's letter to friends in Philippi includes this encouragement to lay aside fear by trusting in Christ.

Read Philippians 1-4.

Romans 8:15

 For ye have not received the spirit of bondage again to fear; but ye have received the Spirit of adoption, whereby we cry, Abba, Father. (KJV)

 For you didn't receive a spirit of bondage to fear, but you received the Spirit of adoption, by whom we cry, "Abba! Father!" (WEB)

My Favorite Bible Translation of this Verse:

Pause to Ponder

Doodle . Draw . Write . Doodle . Draw . Write

Who?

What?

When?

Where?

Why?

How?

What if?

Consider the Context

Paul's letter to the Romans includes words about life through the Spirit.

Read Romans 8:1-17.

2 Timothy 1:7

 For God hath not given us the spirit of fear; but of power, love, and of a sound mind. (KJV)

 For God didn't give us a spirit of fear, but of power, love, and self-control. (WEB)

My Favorite Bible Translation of this Verse:

Pause to Ponder

Doodle . Draw . Write . Doodle . Draw . Write

Who?

What?

When?

Where?

Why?

How?

What if?

Consider the Context

In 2 Timothy, Paul encourages his young protege Timothy to be a faithful leader.

Read 2 Timothy 2:1 - 3:26.

1 John 4:18

 There is no fear in love; but perfect love casteth out fear: because fear hath torment. He that feareth is not made perfect in love. (KJV)

 There is no fear in love; but perfect love casts out fear, because fear has punishment. He who fears is not made perfect in love. (WEB)

My Favorite Bible Translation of this Verse:

Pause to Ponder

Doodle . Draw . Write . Doodle . Draw . Write

Who?

What?

When?

Where?

Why?

How?

What if?

Consider the Context

Written by the Apostle John, 1 John has a great emphasis on love for God and for others.

Read 1 John 4:7-21.

Hang On Or Hand It Over

The first step to dealing with fear and anxiety is to acknowledge it's there. Then, there's a decision to be made: hang on to it or hand it over to the LORD.

Hebrews 4:16: "Let us therefore come boldly unto the throne of grace, that we may obtain mercy, and find grace to help in time of need."

Sometimes, I imagine taking my fear and putting in a basket. I pick up the basket and carry it into a beautiful, heavenly throne room where the Father and Son are sitting side by side on a throne. I carry the basket (or if it's particularly heavy, I may have to drag it like a ball and chain) across the throne room floor. There, I leave it to rest at Jesus' feet.

Not all fears and anxieties carry the same weight, but I've found that refusing to lay them down or ask for help in carrying them can take a tremendous toll on my mental, spiritual, relational, and even physical health.

In a fitness class one day, my friend and instructor, Suzi, said, "You need light weights for our workout today."

I'm glad I fought the urge to pick up heavier weights, because she led us in a series of seemingly simple exercises where we had to hold those feather light weights for a long, long time...using one tiny repetitive movement. It was astounding how simple little movements became more and more difficult with every passing minute.

Why? Because even if weights are light, the longer you hold them, the heavier they become.

Our fears and anxieties are like that- the longer we hold them, the heavier they grow.

Here are some self-evaluation questions I've found helpful in dealing with my fears:

- Have I been holding on to a certain fear?
- What's the name of my fear?
- Have I been harboring a particular anxiety?
- Is it time for me to lay it down?
- Is it time for me to ask for help in carrying this burden?

I encourage you to stop trying to carry your concerns all by yourself. Look at this beautiful invitation we have to unload our worries found in 1 Peter 5:6-7.

"Humble yourselves therefore under the mighty hand of God, that he may exalt you in due time; casting all your worries on him, because he cares for you."

He. Cares. For. You.

God can be trusted to be strong and wise enough to carry our concerns—all of them.

1 Peter 5:7

 Casting all your care upon him; for he careth for you. (KJV)

 Cast all your anxiety on him because he cares for you. (WEB)

My Favorite Bible Translation of this Verse:

Pause to Ponder

Doodle . Draw . Write . Doodle . Draw . Write

Who?

What?

When?

Where?

Why?

How?

What if?

Consider the Context

Peter's words to church leaders are found in 1 Peter.

Read 1 Peter 5:1-11.

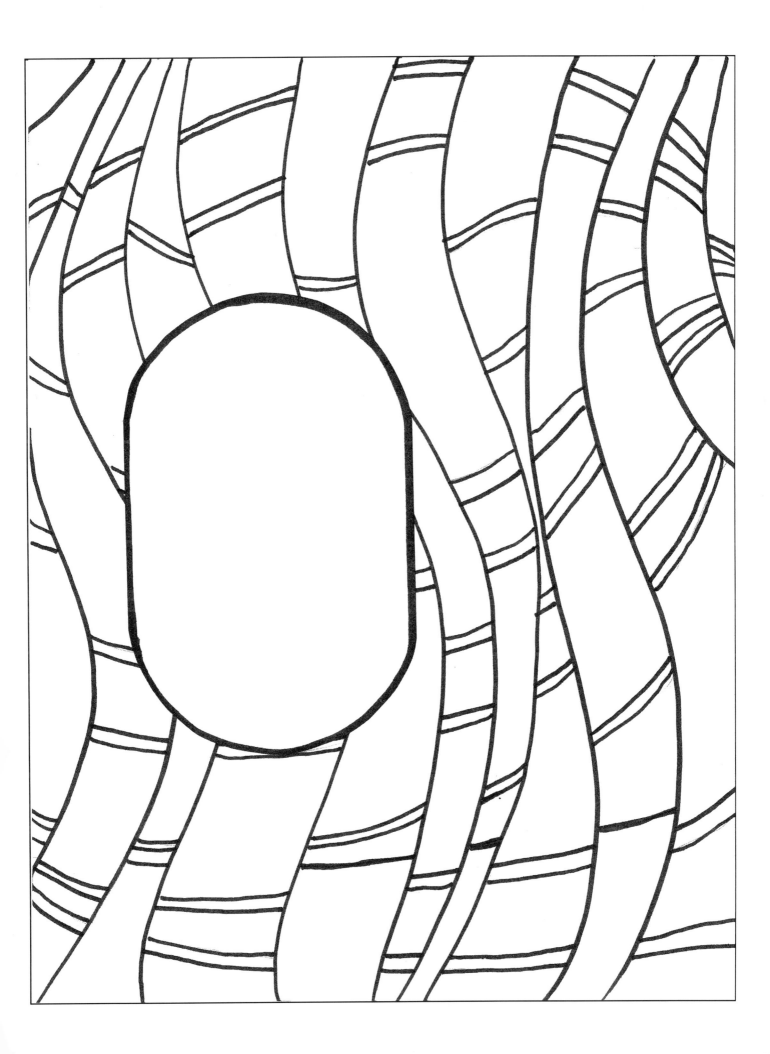

Proverbs 12:25

 Heaviness in the heart of man maketh it stoop: but a good word maketh it glad. (KJV)

 Anxiety in a man's heart weighs it down, but a kind word makes it glad. (WEB)

My Favorite Bible Translation of this Verse:

Pause to Ponder

Doodle . Draw . Write . Doodle . Draw . Write

Who?

What?

When?

Where?

Why?

How?

What if?

Consider the Context

There are 31 chapters in Proverbs. Most were written by Solomon, the wisest man who ever lived. Read one chapter a day for a daily dose of God's wisdom!

Read Proverbs 12.

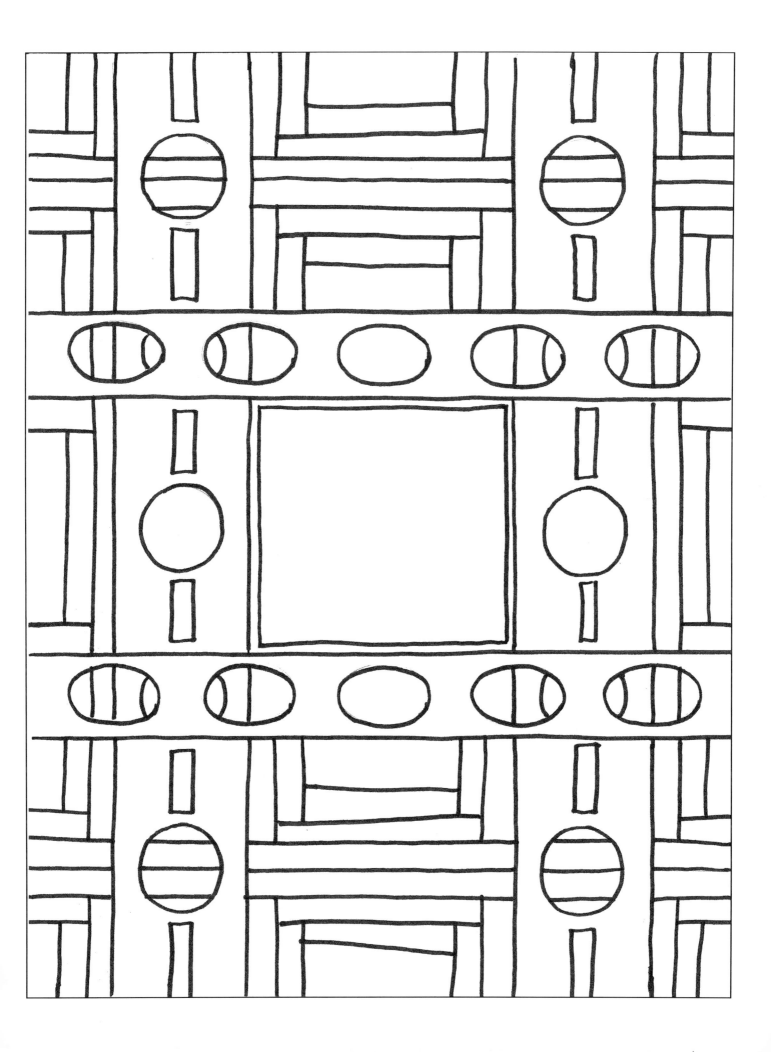

Ecclesiastes 11:10

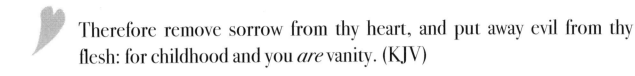

Therefore remove sorrow from thy heart, and put away evil from thy flesh: for childhood and you *are* vanity. (KJV)

Therefore remove sorrow from your heart, and put away evil from your flesh; for youth and the dawn of life are vanity. (WEB)

My Favorite Bible Translation of this Verse:

Pause to Ponder

Doodle . Draw . Write . Doodle . Draw . Write

Who?

What?

When?

Where?

Why?

How?

What if?

Consider the Context

Written by Solomon, he encourages us to remember our Creator while we are young.

Read Ecclesiastes 11:7 - 12:8.

Psalm 94:19

 In the multitude of my thoughts within me thy comforts delight my soul. (KJV)

 In the multitude of my thoughts within me, your comforts delight my soul. (WEB)

My Favorite Bible Translation of this Verse:

Pause to Ponder

Doodle . Draw . Write . Doodle . Draw . Write

Who?

What?

When?

Where?

Why?

How?

What if?

Consider the Context

Psalm 94 is a cry to God to rise up and avenge wrongs suffered at the hands of others.

Read Psalm 94:1-23.

1 Peter 3:14

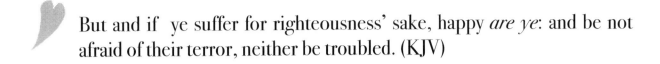 But and if ye suffer for righteousness' sake, happy *are ye*: and be not afraid of their terror, neither be troubled. (KJV)

But even if you should suffer for righteousness' sake, you are blessed. "Don't fear what they fear, neither be troubled." (WEB)

My Favorite Bible Translation of this Verse:

Pause to Ponder

Doodle . Draw . Write . Doodle . Draw . Write

Who?

What?

When?

Where?

Why?

How?

What if?

Consider the Context

Read Peter's passage about suffering for doing good found in 1 Peter 3.

Read 1 Peter 3:8-22.

Luke 2:10

 And the angel said unto them, Fear not: for, behold I bring you good tidings of great joy, which shall be to all people. (KJV)

 The angel said to them, "Don't be afraid, for behold, I bring you good news of great joy which will be to all the people." (WEB)

My Favorite Bible Translation of this Verse:

Pause to Ponder

Doodle . Draw . Write . Doodle . Draw . Write

Who?

What?

When?

Where?

Why?

How?

What if?

Consider the Context

The night angels appeared to shepherds announcing Jesus' birth, the shepherds were terrified. The message they were given? Do not fear!

Read Luke 2:1-20.

Joshua 1:9

 Have not I commanded thee? Be strong and of a good courage; be not afraid, neither be thou dismayed: for the LORD thy God *is* with thee whithersoever thou goest. (KJV)

 Haven't I commanded you? Be strong and courageous. Don't be afraid, neither be dismayed: for Yahweh your God is with you wherever you go. (WEB)

My Favorite Bible Translation of this Verse:

Pause to Ponder

Doodle . Draw . Write . Doodle . Draw . Write

Who?

What?

When?

Where?

Why?

How?

What if?

Consider the Context

The mantle of leadership for the Hebrew people has been passed from Moses to Joshua. Joshua is on the brink of leading the people of Israel into the promised land.

Read Joshua 1:1-9.

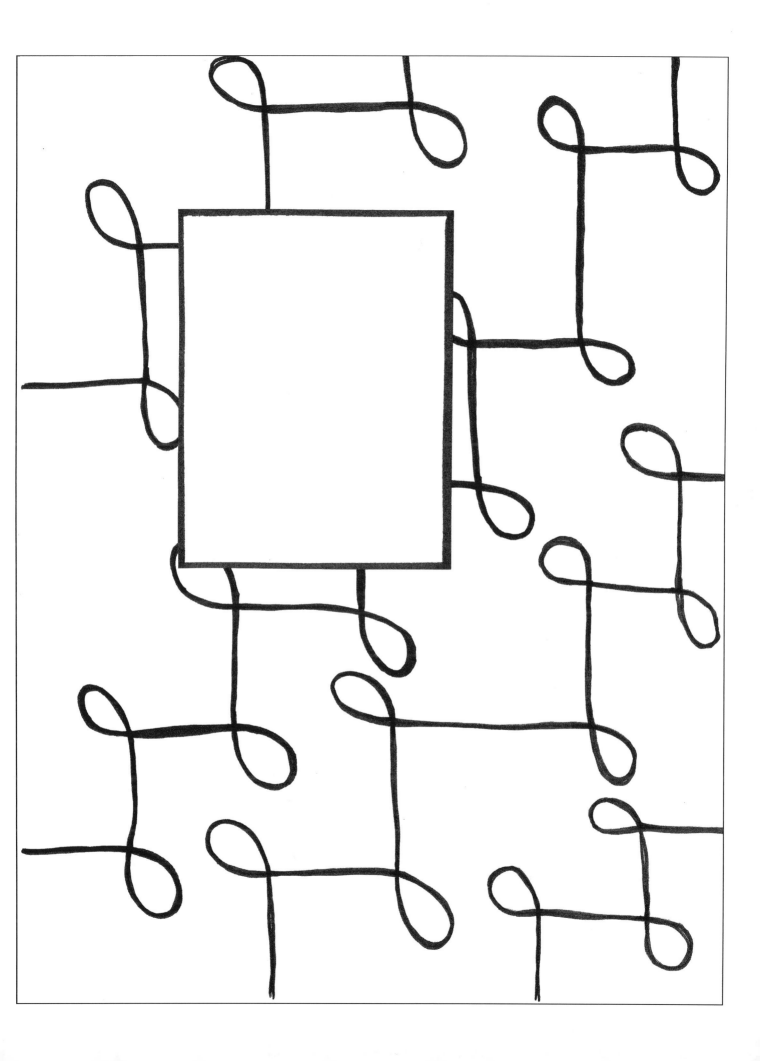

About the Author / Artist

Debbie Hannah Skinner

Debbie Hannah Skinner is an artist, author, and Bible teacher who delights in helping women engage their hands in art as a way to focus their hearts on God.

She speaks nationally with a Bible in one hand and watercolor brush in the other, painting as she presents to women's groups. Debbie inspires women to paint the world around them with the beautiful colors of hope and help they discover in Scripture.

Debbie especially loves to help women who think they are *non-artists* discover the joy of using watercolor art as a vibrant expression of faith. (Though artists are certainly invited to join in the fun as well!)

Founder of WisdomInWatercolor.com, Debbie specializes in the use of watercolor paints and pencils for Bible journaling, prayer journaling, and Scripture meditation. Her paintings have been published nationally and her prints are available online at her ImageKind gallery.

Visit Debbie's online print gallery:
DebbieHannahSkinner.ImageKind.com

Connect with Debbie at:
WisdomInWatercolor.com

Book Debbie for a Speaking Event or
a Color Through the Bible Workshop:
ChristianSpeakersServices.com/debbiehannahskinner.html

More Books By Debbie Hannah Skinner

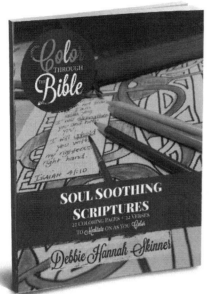

Soul Soothing Scriptures

Debbie's first contemplative coloring book, *Soul Soothing Scriptures* (Color Through the Bible, Volume 1), contains 22 coloring pages and 22 scriptures to mediate on as you color.

Hope Is Always Near

Hope Is Always Near weaves

together Bible verses about hope with accompanying quotes. Debbie's paintings serve as the backdrop and there's space to doodle throughout and journal in the back. It's Debbie's hope you find encouragement through *Hope Is Always Near* and that you share it with people you love. *Hope Is Always Near* is a colorful gift book that uses Debbie's words and paintings alongside selected Scriptures to speak to our longing for hope in a world that sometimes feels hopeless.

To order a copy, visit:
WisdomInWatercolor.com/book-store

Also available at other online bookstores such as:
Amazon, Barnes and Noble, Books-a-Million, and IndieBound

Stay Connected

Want to know more? To learn about
upcoming volumes of this coloring book series
plus
Debbie's online art classes & other resources,
please visit

ColorThroughTheBible.com

Website: WisdomInWatercolor.com
Facebook: ColorThroughTheBibleScriptureSavors

Play Ground

Use this area to test your markers or colors before applying them to a page.

Made in the USA
Columbia, SC
15 August 2019